ACKNOWLEDGEMENTS

"Word of the Day" was created by the inspiration of my teacher, The Holy Spirit. It was created to serve as a life lesson to all who feel like they have done too much to be forgiven. God is willing and able to save and forgive. Throughout this journey, the Holy Spirit will remind you of the merciful God we serve.

To my late parents and brother, Ethel Romar Hopkins, Jacob Williams, Harry Lee Hopkins and Darren Jacob Williams thank you for who you were in my life. I hope I've made you proud.

To my husband, James Jackson, you've been my rock for 30+ plus years when no one understood your assignment you were still there. Thank you for being patient in my growth.

To my children and grandchild Ty Jackson, Reynaud Jackson, and Jamir Bookman all that I do, I do with you in mind. Thank you for believing in me.

To my great aunt Josephine " Minnie" Irving, who always has a "Gooo Get'em, Girl" in her spirit to offer me. Thank you!

To my circle of brains and beauty Melinda Jackson, Erika Jackson, Kayla Jackson, and Yana Rue thank you for all your help and words of encouragement. It was a humbling experience being vulnerable while birthing what God has given me.

To my Igniting God's Vision Ministries, Inc family thank you for your prayers and encouragement.

To the prophet that delivered the word about this journey, Bishop Dr. Floyd Smith, thank you! Even though I laughed at him as Sarah laughed at the news of birthing a child at 90, yet he prayed, labored, and encouraged me.

To my family and everyone that has ever been in my circle of influence past or present, whether you were a lesson or a blessing, know that I have learned from each of you and as I continue becoming who God has called me to be, those life lessons will always be with me and for that I am grateful. Thank you!

Last but not least to my big brother Brian Williams, my "You Got This" guy, thank you!

LET'S WRITE A NEW THING WITH OUR WORDS!

POWER OF WORDS

THE WORD OF GOD MATTERS!

Your WORDS Matter!

Let's take a brief look at the power of words in both the first book of the old testament and the new testament.

God spoke Words to create the world. *Genesis 1:1-31*
The WORD(God) gave His WORD (Jesus) to change the world. *John 1:1-18*

As you begin to write and pray, be mindful of how much your words matter.

Words you speak over yourselves matter!
Words you speak over your workplace and boss matter!
Words you speak over your government and people in authority matter!
Words you speak over your children matter!
Words you speak and come into agreement with over your health matter!
Words you speak over your leaders and ministries matter!
Words you speak over your loved ones matter!
Words you speak over the person that cut you off in traffic matter!
Words you speak over your mates and relationships matter!
Words you speak over your current situation matters!

I think we understand now that **EVERY** word matters!

Words we read, hear, and speak are vying for control of our mind, will, and emotions (our soul).

We are speaking word curses over many things because we are not grasping the power God has given us. The enemy is elated at our ignorance of the power we possess.

YOUR WORDS ARE YOUR EXPRESSED THOUGHTS THAT CREATE LIFE AND DEATH!

WARNING!!
WARNING!!
WARNING!!

THIS JOURNAL CONTAINS VERY SHORT, POWERFUL, PERSONAL PRAYERS INTENDED TO CHANGE *YOU* NOT OTHERS AROUND YOU!

Word of the Day
Part 4

Introduction

This experience is to encourage you to keep your thoughts towards the Lord daily and to do it with your speech, attitude, and your spiritual walk-in mind.

Throughout the bible, it instructs us about the Word of God and the importance of knowing it for yourself. *Be diligent to present yourself approved to God, a worker who does not need to be ashamed, rightly dividing the word of truth. 2 Timothy 2:15.* Take time to dig deeper into each of the words as you journal and let it resonate and take root.

The WORD is GOD; therefore, it is not much you can do successfully or peacefully apart from it. To live in the will of God, you must know what the will of the Father is for your life, which is found only in His Word. Nothing is more important in your spiritual growth than to know His Word. *In the beginning, was the Word, and the Word was with God, and the Word was God. John 1:1*

To be used by God effectively we must be equipped for the work. *All Scripture is given by inspiration of God and is profitable for doctrine, for reproof, for correction, for instruction in righteousness, that the man of God may be complete, thoroughly equipped for every good work. 2 Timothy 3:16.*

This journal is designed to highlight a word daily that will challenge you on your spiritual journey. The first week you will focus on the importance of God's Word and His instructions. Every 7th day you will be challenged to meditate on the fullness of God and the words from the prior week. Every two weeks you will be challenged to step outside your comfort zone and do things you've possibly never done.
As you read daily and fully participate in this journaling experience, I pray the words the Holy Spirit has given me will encourage you to grow spiritually, allow change to come forth and your soul to be stirred!

I pray your hearts and minds are open to receive what the Lord has to say as journaling will open your heart to God in a very personal way.

As you read and journal you will gain insight into some things that may be a hindrance to your next level. When you've complete parts 1-4, you will have completed the entire 365 journal experience! LET'S CONTINUE!

ASSIGNMENT

The Lord knew that David would fail miserably, but
that he would still fulfill His will.

Don't allow what man think or say keep you licking healed wounds!
Get back to your kingdom assignment!

PSALM 103:10-14
2 SAMUEL 11

How did this word speak to you today?

_____

_____

_____

_____

_____

_____

_____

_____

_____

_____

_____

_____

_____

_____

_____

_____

_____

_____

_____

_____

_____

CHALLENGE

Today I challenge you to call or visit or elderly
a family member or neighbor.

HEBREWS 10:24-25

Were you comfortable with the challenge? Why or why not?

_____

_____

_____

_____

_____

_____

_____

_____

_____

_____

_____

_____

_____

_____

_____

_____

_____

_____

_____

_____

_____

_____

_____

Day 3

THIRST

Only you, dear Lord can quench my thirst and fill the void in my life.
Fill me with your spirit until I overflow.
In the Name of Jesus. Amen.

PSALM 63:1

Did this word bring you to a place of reflection?

_____
_____
_____
_____
_____
_____
_____
_____
_____
_____
_____
_____
_____
_____
_____
_____
_____
_____
_____
_____
_____
_____
_____

SUSTAIN

Thank you, Father, for restoring the joy of your salvation and granting
me a willing spirit to sustain me. Strengthen me so I can teach
transgressors your ways, so that sinners will turn back to you.
In the Name of Jesus. Amen.

PSALM 51:12-13

Did the Holy Spirit speak to that place in your heart?

_____

_____

_____

_____

_____

_____

_____

_____

_____

_____

_____

_____

_____

_____

_____

_____

_____

_____

_____

_____

_____

Day 5

CONTINUOUSLY

Lord, keep me in a place of worship. May I
continuously water my garden of victories.
In the Name of Jesus. Amen.

LUKE 4:8

Declare the blessings of the Lord over your life today as you journal.

_____

_____

_____

_____

_____

_____

_____

_____

_____

_____

_____

_____

_____

_____

_____

_____

_____

_____

_____

_____

_____

MEDITATE

Today I will discipline myself to meditate for 5 minutes on the fullness of God and how He is showing Himself mighty in my life through His Word.

PHILIPPIANS 4:8

Your thoughts, prayers or questions about this time with the Lord;

_____

_____

_____

_____

_____

_____

_____

_____

_____

_____

_____

_____

_____

_____

_____

_____

_____

_____

_____

_____

_____

Day 7

DISCERN

**Inside every person you know, there's a person you don't know.
Keep Watch!**

Beloved, do not believe every spirit but test the spirits, whether they are of God.
1 JOHN 4:1

What did the Holy Spirit reveal to you from this reading?

_____

_____

_____

_____

_____

_____

_____

_____

_____

_____

_____

_____

_____

_____

_____

_____

_____

_____

_____

_____

_____

WILL

Father, I desire to do your will. Your law is within my heart.
Let your will be done on earth as it is in heaven.
In the Name of Jesus. Amen.

PSALM 40:8

Take a moment and reflect on today's word before journaling.

_____

_____

_____

_____

_____

_____

_____

_____

_____

_____

_____

_____

_____

_____

_____

_____

_____

_____

_____

_____

_____

_____

POWER

I will still blossom in the face of trials because
God's power is at work within me.
In the Name of Jesus. Amen.

2 CORINTHIANS 4:7

Were you comforted by this word?

_____

_____

_____

_____

_____

_____

_____

_____

_____

_____

_____

_____

_____

_____

_____

_____

_____

_____

_____

_____

_____

_____

_____

_____

ENLIGHTENED

Today my Lord, I pray the eyes of my understanding
be enlightened; that I may know what is the hope of your calling.
In the Name of Jesus. Amen.

EPHESIANS 1:18

What did the Holy Spirit reveal to you from this reading?

_____

_____

_____

_____

_____

_____

_____

_____

_____

_____

_____

_____

_____

_____

_____

_____

_____

_____

_____

_____

_____

_____

_____

BETTER

Because Your lovingkindness is better than life,
my lips shall praise You forever.
In Jesus Name. Amen.

PSALM 34:4-5

How did this word speak to you today?

_____

_____

_____

_____

_____

_____

_____

_____

_____

_____

_____

_____

_____

_____

_____

_____

_____

_____

_____

_____

_____

_____

_____

_____

_____

Day 12

TRICKS

Lord, keep me on spiritual watch at all times. The tricks of the enemy are so easily overlooked in my natural sight but with your Holy Spirit, I will be made aware. In the Name of Jesus. Amen.

1 PETER 5:8-9

What did you learn about yourself from this word?

_____

_____

_____

_____

_____

_____

_____

_____

_____

_____

_____

_____

_____

_____

_____

_____

_____

_____

_____

_____

MEDITATE

Today I will discipline myself to meditate for 5 minutes on the fullness of God and how He is showing Himself mighty in my life through His Word.

PHILIPPIANS 4:8

Your thoughts, prayers or questions about this time with the Lord;

_____

_____

_____

_____

_____

_____

_____

_____

_____

_____

_____

_____

_____

_____

_____

_____

_____

_____

_____

_____

_____

_____

_____

SEEK

Seek the scriptures for instructions on how to
live your best life for real. Not just for
man, or social media.
LIVE YOUR TRUTH! THERE YOU WILL FIND PEACE.

1 PETER 3:8-12

What did the Holy Spirit reveal to you from this reading?

_____

_____

_____

_____

_____

_____

_____

_____

_____

_____

_____

_____

_____

_____

_____

_____

_____

_____

_____

_____

_____

_____

_____

GLORY

Father, never let me think of myself as more than I should.
May the gifts you have gifted me always be used for your glory.
In the Name of Jesus. Amen.

PROVERBS 27:2

Read and reflect on this scripture today as you journal.

_____

_____

_____

_____

_____

_____

_____

_____

_____

_____

_____

_____

_____

_____

_____

_____

_____

_____

_____

_____

_____

_____

_____

_____

Day 16

CHALLENGE

Today I challenge you to offer the free gift of salvation. Romans10:9-10

HEBREWS 10:24-25

Were you comfortable with the challenge? Why or why not?

_____

_____

_____

_____

_____

_____

_____

_____

_____

_____

_____

_____

_____

_____

_____

_____

_____

_____

_____

_____

_____

_____

Day 17

PERFECT

Thank you, Father, for your strength and anointing that
is being made perfect in me for the work of your kingdom.
In the Name of Jesus. Amen.

2 CORINTHIANS 12:9

Were you comforted by this word?

DELIGHT

Father, even when trouble and distress come upon me,
your commands still give me delight.
In the Name of Jesus. Amen.

Hallelujah!

PSALM 119:43

Read and reflect on this scripture today as you journal.

_____

_____

_____

_____

_____

_____

_____

_____

_____

_____

_____

_____

_____

_____

_____

_____

_____

_____

_____

_____

_____

_____

Day 19

SEE

Thank you, Father, that you have opened my eyes that I
may see wonderful things in your law.

PSALM 119:18

What did the Holy Spirit reveal to you from this reading?

_____

_____

_____

_____

_____

_____

_____

_____

_____

_____

_____

_____

_____

_____

_____

_____

_____

_____

_____

_____

MEDITATE

Today I will discipline myself to meditate for 5 minutes on the fullness of God
and how He is showing Himself mighty in my life through His Word.

PHILIPPIANS 4:8

Your thoughts, prayers or questions about this time with the Lord;

_____
_____
_____
_____
_____
_____
_____
_____
_____
_____
_____
_____
_____
_____
_____
_____
_____
_____
_____
_____
_____
_____

Day 21

HEARTACHE

One thing you can't hide from on this side of heaven
is heartache. Trust God to sooth every area of hurt.
Thank you, Father, for our comforter, Jesus.

MATTHEW 5:4

Were you comforted by this word?

_____
_____
_____
_____
_____
_____
_____
_____
_____
_____
_____
_____
_____
_____
_____
_____
_____
_____
_____
_____
_____
_____
_____

Day 22

IMPERFECT

I am perfectly imperfect, standing in need of
God's grace, mercy, and forgiveness daily.

Exodus 34:6-7

How did today's reading impact you?

_____
_____
_____
_____
_____
_____
_____
_____
_____
_____
_____
_____
_____
_____
_____
_____
_____
_____
_____
_____
_____
_____

CHAINED

Your mind may be chained.
Your physical body may be chained.
But God's word will never be chained.
**It shall accomplish God's will.
BELIEVE!**

2 TIMOTHY 2:9

Were you comforted by this word?

_____

_____

_____

_____

_____

_____

_____

_____

_____

_____

_____

_____

_____

_____

_____

_____

_____

_____

_____

_____

_____

_____

HYPOCRITES

Lord, I will seek you daily and I honor you with my life.
In the Name of Jesus. Amen.

*These people honor me with their lips, but their hearts are far from me.
They worship me in vain; their teachings are merely human rules.*
MATTHEW 15:19

Did the Holy Spirit speak to that place in your heart?

_____

_____

_____

_____

_____

_____

_____

_____

_____

_____

_____

_____

_____

_____

_____

_____

_____

_____

_____

_____

_____

_____

ABUNDANCE

God is not a God of just enough!
God is a God of abundance!
Everything under the heavens belongs to Him!
What are you in need of?

Proverb 3:10

Declare the blessings of the Lord over your life today as you journal.

ENTER

I will enter your gates with thanksgiving and your courts with praise; I give thanks to you Father, and praise Your name.
HALLELUJAH!

PSALM 100:1-5

Take a moment and reflect on today's word before journaling.

_____

_____

_____

_____

_____

_____

_____

_____

_____

_____

_____

_____

_____

_____

_____

_____

_____

_____

_____

_____

_____

_____

_____

MEDITATE

Today I will discipline myself to meditate for 5 minutes on the fullness of God and how He is showing Himself mighty in my life through His Word.

PHILIPPIANS 4:8

Your thoughts, prayers or questions about this time with the Lord;

_____

_____

_____

_____

_____

_____

_____

_____

_____

_____

_____

_____

_____

_____

_____

_____

_____

_____

_____

_____

_____

_____

_____

_____

FEAR

The Spirit of the knowledge and fear of the Lord Is upon Jesus.
May I always be in a place of respect and honor of you Lord.
In the Name of Jesus. Amen.

ISAIAH 11:3

How did this word speak to you today?

_____

_____

_____

_____

_____

_____

_____

_____

_____

_____

_____

_____

_____

_____

_____

_____

_____

_____

_____

_____

_____

_____

Day 29

WHATEVER

Jesus, I pray, whatever I do, whether in word or deed, I do
it all in your name, giving thanks to God the Father through you.
In Jesus Name. Amen.

COLOSSIANS 3:17

What did the Holy Spirit reveal to you from this reading?

_____

_____

_____

_____

_____

_____

_____

_____

_____

_____

_____

_____

_____

_____

_____

_____

_____

_____

_____

_____

_____

_____

_____

CHALLENGE

Today I challenge you to call someone you haven't
spoken to and offer to pray with them.

HEBREWS 10:24-25

Were you comfortable with the challenge? Why or why not?

_____

_____

_____

_____

_____

_____

_____

_____

_____

_____

_____

_____

_____

_____

_____

_____

_____

_____

_____

_____

_____

_____

_____

_____

THANKS

I give thanks to you LORD, for you are good. Your love endures
forever. I will exalt, magnify, and glorify you always!
In the Name of Jesus. Amen.

PSALM 136:1-3

Take a moment and reflect on today's word before journaling.

_____

_____

_____

_____

_____

_____

_____

_____

_____

_____

_____

_____

_____

_____

_____

_____

_____

_____

_____

_____

_____

_____

MONTH 11

YOUR COMMITMENT IS COMENDABLE!

CONGRATULATIONS!

PRAISE THE LORD!

WORK

Even if your platform is not the pulpit,
you still have work to do!!
Someone is watching...
Someone is waiting...
Someone is ready...
Someone is hungry...
Someone is desperate...
FOR YOU TO GET IT RIGHT!
Their very life depends upon you getting to work!

JOHN 9:4

Did the Holy Spirit speak to that place in your heart?

_____

_____

_____

_____

_____

_____

_____

_____

_____

_____

_____

_____

_____

_____

_____

_____

_____

_____

_____

Day 33

LIE

"God is not a man, that He should lie,
Nor a son of man, that He should repent.
Has He said, and will He not do?
Or has He spoken, and will He not make it good?
NUMBERS 23:19

Read and reflect on this scripture today as you journal.

MEDITATE

Today I will discipline myself to meditate for 5 minutes on the fullness of God and how He is showing Himself mighty in my life through His Word.

PHILIPPIANS 4:8

Your thoughts, prayers or questions about this time with the Lord;

_____

_____

_____

_____

_____

_____

_____

_____

_____

_____

_____

_____

_____

_____

_____

_____

_____

_____

_____

_____

_____

_____

_____

_____

REWARD

Lord, when I give to the needy, I pray my motives are pure and with you in mind. Understanding my reward comes from you and you only.
In the Name of Jesus. Amen.

MATTHEW 6:3-4

Take a moment and reflect on today's word before journaling.

_____

_____

_____

_____

_____

_____

_____

_____

_____

_____

_____

_____

_____

_____

_____

_____

_____

_____

_____

_____

FRUIT

Father, on the day of accountability, when you ask me to show the fruit of your bountiful provisions that you have given me, I pray that you will be pleased. Continue to mold me as I move as Christ moves.
In the Name of Jesus. Amen.

LUKE 12:48

What did the Holy Spirit reveal to you from this reading?

_____

_____

_____

_____

_____

_____

_____

_____

_____

_____

_____

_____

_____

_____

_____

_____

_____

_____

_____

_____

_____

_____

JUDGE

Lord, may I judge myself in truth, that I would not be judged. Teach
me to judge my thoughts and actions according to your word.
In the Name of Jesus. Amen.

1 CORINTHIANS 11:31

How did this word speak to you today?

_____

_____

_____

_____

_____

_____

_____

_____

_____

_____

_____

_____

_____

_____

_____

_____

_____

_____

_____

_____

_____

_____

_____

ANOINTING

When God called you to do a thing, He has also gifted you the anointing to do it.
Others can go through the motions of doing it but God's power is
backing you when you do it. Someone or something is waiting
for you to walk in your anointing.

JOHN 14:6

Did the Holy Spirit speak to that place in your heart?

_____

_____

_____

_____

_____

_____

_____

_____

_____

_____

_____

_____

_____

_____

_____

_____

_____

_____

_____

_____

_____

_____

_____

BORN

Very truly I tell you, no one can enter the kingdom of God
unless they are born of water and the Spirit.
Flesh gives birth to flesh, but the Spirit
gives birth to spirit.
JOHN 3:5-6

How did this word speak to you today?

_____

_____

_____

_____

_____

_____

_____

_____

_____

_____

_____

_____

_____

_____

_____

_____

_____

_____

_____

_____

_____

_____

MASTER

For sin shall no longer be my master, because
I am not under the law but grace.
In the Name of Jesus. Amen.

HALLELUJAH!

ROMANS 6:14

Did the Holy Spirit speak to that place in your heart where you are struggling?

_____

_____

_____

_____

_____

_____

_____

_____

_____

_____

_____

_____

_____

_____

_____

_____

_____

_____

_____

_____

_____

_____

_____

MEDITATE

Today I will discipline myself to meditate for 5 minutes on the fullness of God and how He is showing Himself mighty in my life through His Word.

PHILIPPIANS 4:8

Your thoughts, prayers or questions about this time with the Lord;

_____

_____

_____

_____

_____

_____

_____

_____

_____

_____

_____

_____

_____

_____

_____

_____

_____

_____

_____

_____

_____

_____

_____

_____

FLESH

For my flesh desires what is contrary to the Spirit, and the Spirit what is
contrary to the flesh. Lord, I pray your word sustains me in
these times so I may align my flesh with your word.
In the Name of Jesus. Amen.

GALATIANS 5:17-21

Look into yourself, do your flesh pose an issue in your daily walk?

_____

_____

_____

_____

_____

_____

_____

_____

_____

_____

_____

_____

_____

_____

_____

_____

_____

_____

_____

_____

Day 43

WILDERNESS

For only you Lord, have the power to make a way in the wilderness and
streams in the wasteland. Only you Lord, will I follow.
In the Name of Jesus. Amen.

ISAIAH 43:19

What did the Holy Spirit reveal to you from this reading?

_____

_____

_____

_____

_____

_____

_____

_____

_____

_____

_____

_____

_____

_____

_____

_____

_____

_____

_____

CHALLENGE

Today I challenge you to donate
clothing you no longer
wear to a charity.

HEBREWS 10:24-25

Were you comfortable with the challenge? Why or why not?

_____

_____

_____

_____

_____

_____

_____

_____

_____

_____

_____

_____

_____

_____

_____

_____

_____

_____

_____

_____

_____

_____

_____

ABOVE

Lord, teach me to love you above all else!
In the Name of Jesus. Amen.

PSALM 143:8

What did the Holy Spirit reveal to you from this reading?

_____

_____

_____

_____

_____

_____

_____

_____

_____

_____

_____

_____

_____

_____

_____

_____

_____

_____

_____

_____

_____

_____

_____

PLANS

Father, may I not cling to what is familiar or my past
accomplishments, but to the plans you have for my future.
In the Name of Jesus. Amen.

JEREMIAH 29:11

Write affirmations for your life today.

_____

_____

_____

_____

_____

_____

_____

_____

_____

_____

_____

_____

_____

_____

_____

_____

_____

_____

_____

_____

_____

_____

Day 47

TELL

Don't allow people to tell you with their mouth they love you,
but their deeds clearly tell a different story.
Keep Watch!

1 JOHN 3:18

Did the Holy Spirit speak to that place in your heart?

_____

_____

_____

_____

_____

_____

_____

_____

_____

_____

_____

_____

_____

_____

_____

_____

_____

_____

_____

_____

_____

_____

_____

MEDITATE

Today I will discipline myself to meditate for 5 minutes on the fullness of God and how He is showing Himself mighty in my life through His Word.

PHILIPPIANS 4:8

Your thoughts, prayers or questions about this time with the Lord;

_____

_____

_____

_____

_____

_____

_____

_____

_____

_____

_____

_____

_____

_____

_____

_____

_____

_____

_____

_____

_____

_____

_____

TREASURE

Lord, I pray I am forever mindful that I should
lay up my treasures in heaven, not on earth.
In the Name of Jesus. Amen.

MATTHEW 6:19-21

How did this word speak to you today?

_____

_____

_____

_____

_____

_____

_____

_____

_____

_____

_____

_____

_____

_____

_____

_____

_____

_____

_____

_____

_____

_____

Day 50

SOUL

Until your soul is sold out to the will of God, you will continue to get in your own way!
(Your soul is your mind, will, and emotions)

1 KINGS 8:61

What did you learn about yourself from this word?

_____
_____
_____
_____
_____
_____
_____
_____
_____
_____
_____
_____
_____
_____
_____
_____
_____
_____
_____
_____
_____
_____
_____

REST

REST IF YOU MUST, BUT DON'T YOU QUIT!

For my yoke is easy and my burden is light.
MATTHEW 11:28-30

How did today's reading impact you?

_____

_____

_____

_____

_____

_____

_____

_____

_____

_____

_____

_____

_____

_____

_____

_____

_____

_____

_____

_____

_____

_____

_____

REVENGE

THE BEST REVENGE IS NO REVENGE!

Move forward in Christ!

ROMANS 12:19

Were you comforted by this word?

_____

_____

_____

_____

_____

_____

_____

_____

_____

_____

_____

_____

_____

_____

_____

_____

_____

_____

_____

_____

_____

_____

_____

_____

FOOLS

BE MINDFUL OF YOUR WORDS!

The lips of fools bring them strife, and their mouths invite a beating.
PROVERBS 18:6-7

Read and reflect on this scripture today as you journal.

_____

_____

_____

_____

_____

_____

_____

_____

_____

_____

_____

_____

_____

_____

_____

_____

_____

_____

_____

_____

_____

_____

_____

_____

NARROW

I've done things my way and it did not work out as well as I thought.
Lord, I desire to walk on the narrow road which leads to life.
In the Name of Jesus. Amen.

MATTHEW 7:13-14

How did this word speak to you today?

_____

_____

_____

_____

_____

_____

_____

_____

_____

_____

_____

_____

_____

_____

_____

_____

_____

_____

_____

_____

_____

_____

_____

Day 55

MEDITATE

Today I will discipline myself to meditate for 5 minutes on the fullness of God and how He is showing Himself mighty in my life through His Word.

PHILIPPIANS 4:8

Your thoughts, prayers or questions about this time with the Lord;

_____
_____
_____
_____
_____
_____
_____
_____
_____
_____
_____
_____
_____
_____
_____
_____
_____
_____
_____
_____
_____
_____
_____

PREPARED

Father, I receive all that you have for me!
In the Name of Jesus. Amen.

What no eye has seen, what no ear has heard, and what no human mind has conceived, the things God has prepared for those who love him.
1 CORINTHIANS 2:9

Read and reflect on this scripture today as you journal.

Day 57

PURSUE

Thank you, Father, I have found life, prosperity, and honor
because I chose to pursue righteousness and love.
In Jesus Name. Amen.

PROVERBS 21:21

How did this word speak to you today?

_____
_____
_____
_____
_____
_____
_____
_____
_____
_____
_____
_____
_____
_____
_____
_____
_____
_____
_____
_____
_____
_____

CHALLENGE

Today I challenge you to offer to pray with someone.

HEBREWS 10:24-25

Were you comfortable with the challenge? Why or why not?

_____

_____

_____

_____

_____

_____

_____

_____

_____

_____

_____

_____

_____

_____

_____

_____

_____

_____

_____

_____

_____

_____

_____

_____

Day 59

OPINION

Lord, a word from you sets your people free. Teach me not to give my opinion
but only a word from you. They do not need me, they need you.
Tune my ears to hear all you have for them.
In the Name of Jesus. Amen.

JOHN 8:32

What did the Holy Spirit reveal to you from this reading?

_____

_____

_____

_____

_____

_____

_____

_____

_____

_____

_____

_____

_____

_____

_____

_____

_____

_____

_____

_____

_____

_____

_____

JUDGEMENTAL

A judgmental attitude reveals you are prideful and
you don't trust God to judge accordingly.
Seek the heart of God!

MATTHEW 7:2

Take a moment and reflect on today's word before journaling.

_____
_____
_____
_____
_____
_____
_____
_____
_____
_____
_____
_____
_____
_____
_____
_____
_____
_____
_____
_____
_____
_____
_____

Day 61

DESTROYED

As difficult as some of life's situations have been,
I have not been destroyed.
MOVE IN CHRIST!

2 CORINTHIANS 4:7-10

Read and reflect on this scripture today as you journal.

_____

_____

_____

_____

_____

_____

_____

_____

_____

_____

_____

_____

_____

_____

_____

_____

_____

_____

_____

As you begin the final month of your 365 day journaling experience.... Praise God!!

Take a moment to reflect on the Goodness of God through this journey!

Day 62

MEDITATE

Today I will discipline myself to meditate for 5 minutes on the fullness of God and how He is showing Himself mighty in my life through His Word.

PHILIPPIANS 4:8

Your thoughts, prayers or questions about this time with the Lord;

_____
_____
_____
_____
_____
_____
_____
_____
_____
_____
_____
_____
_____
_____
_____
_____
_____
_____
_____
_____
_____
_____

LESSON

As your called servant, God, you have a purpose for every situation in my life. The good, bad, and the ugly. May I receive the lesson you have for me in each! In the Name of Jesus. Amen.

ROMANS 8:28

What did the Holy Spirit reveal to you from this reading?

_____

_____

_____

_____

_____

_____

_____

_____

_____

_____

_____

_____

_____

_____

_____

_____

_____

_____

_____

_____

_____

_____

_____

_____

Day 64

SEPARATE

I am convinced that neither death nor life, neither angels nor demons, neither the present nor the future, nor any powers, neither height nor depth, nor anything else in all creation, will be able to separate us from the love of God that is in Christ Jesus our Lord.
ROMANS 8:38-39

Were you comforted by this word?

_____
_____
_____
_____
_____
_____
_____
_____
_____
_____
_____
_____
_____
_____
_____
_____
_____
_____
_____
_____
_____
_____

SERVE

Father, teach me how to unselfishly give myself to
others for the work of the kingdom.
In the Name of Jesus. Amen.

ROMANS 12:1

Did the Holy Spirit speak to that place in your heart?

_____

_____

_____

_____

_____

_____

_____

_____

_____

_____

_____

_____

_____

_____

_____

_____

_____

_____

_____

_____

_____

_____

_____

BECOMING

When I accepted you, Christ as my Lord and Savior, I accepted that am constantly in a state of becoming who you designed me to be. My work is never done. Lord, I give myself freely to the process you have begun in me. In Jesus Name. Amen.

PHILIPPIANS 1:6

Take a moment and reflect on today's word before journaling.

_____

_____

_____

_____

_____

_____

_____

_____

_____

_____

_____

_____

_____

_____

_____

_____

_____

_____

_____

_____

_____

_____

_____

HOPE

Father, my hope is in you. You will renew my strength. I will soar on wings like eagles; I will run and not grow weary; I will walk and not be faint.
In the Name of Jesus. Amen.

ISAIAH 40:31

Declare the blessings of the Lord over your life today as you journal.

_____

_____

_____

_____

_____

_____

_____

_____

_____

_____

_____

_____

_____

_____

_____

_____

_____

_____

_____

_____

_____

_____

CLOTHED

I delight greatly in you, LORD; my soul rejoices in you, God.
For you have clothed me with garments of salvation
and arrayed me in a robe of your righteousness.
HALLELUJAH!

ISAIAH 61:10

How did this word speak to you today?

_____
_____
_____
_____
_____
_____
_____
_____
_____
_____
_____
_____
_____
_____
_____
_____
_____
_____
_____
_____
_____
_____
_____

Day 69

MEDITATE

Today I will discipline myself to meditate for 5 minutes on the fullness of God and how He is showing Himself mighty in my life through His Word.

PHILIPPIANS 4:8

Your thoughts, prayers or questions about this time with the Lord;

_____

_____

_____

_____

_____

_____

_____

_____

_____

_____

_____

_____

_____

_____

_____

_____

_____

_____

_____

_____

_____

_____

_____

COVER

Lord, cover and fill every person that seeks you,
needs you, desires you and believes
in you with your precious blood.
In the Name of Jesus. Amen.

HEBREWS 11:6

What did the Holy Spirit reveal to you from this reading?

_____

_____

_____

_____

_____

_____

_____

_____

_____

_____

_____

_____

_____

_____

_____

_____

_____

_____

_____

_____

Day 71

COUNSEL

The Spirit of counsel and might is upon Jesus.
Bring your situation before the perfect counselor!
His guidance in like no other!

ISAIAH 11:2

How did this word speak to you today?

Day 72

CHALLENGE

Today I challenge you to give a gift of love.

HEBREWS 10:24-25

Your thoughts, prayers or questions about today's experience;

_____
_____
_____
_____
_____
_____
_____
_____
_____
_____
_____
_____
_____
_____
_____
_____
_____
_____
_____
_____
_____
_____
_____

SECURE

I'm convinced that nothing is more secure or certain
then the things I entrust to you, Lord.
In the Name of Jesus. Amen.

HALLELUJAH!

Psalm 34:4-5

Were you comforted by this word?

_____

_____

_____

_____

_____

_____

_____

_____

_____

_____

_____

_____

_____

_____

_____

_____

_____

_____

_____

_____

_____

_____

DEEP

Don't be so deep that you can't reach,
somebody, nobody or anybody.
Move-in Christ! Stay Humble!

LUKE 12:2

What did the Holy Spirit reveal to you from this reading?

_____

_____

_____

_____

_____

_____

_____

_____

_____

_____

_____

_____

_____

_____

_____

_____

_____

_____

_____

_____

_____

_____

FREE

The very thing that you are trying to convince yourself you don't
care about, is the very thing you care about the most.
Deal with the issue in Christ!
Get Free! Stay Free!

2 CORINTHIANS 3:17

What did you learn about yourself from this word?

_____

_____

_____

_____

_____

_____

_____

_____

_____

_____

_____

_____

_____

_____

_____

_____

_____

_____

_____

_____

_____

_____

_____

MEDITATE

Today I will discipline myself to meditate for 5 minutes on the fullness of God and how He is showing Himself mighty in my life through His Word.

PHILIPPIANS 4:8

Your thoughts, prayers or questions about this time with the Lord;

_____

_____

_____

_____

_____

_____

_____

_____

_____

_____

_____

_____

_____

_____

_____

_____

_____

_____

_____

_____

_____

_____

_____

_____

JOYFUL

Lord, may I be joyful in hope, patient in
affections and faithful in prayer, always.
In Jesus Name. Amen.

ROMANS 12:12

Declare the word of the Lord over your life today.

_____
_____
_____
_____
_____
_____
_____
_____
_____
_____
_____
_____
_____
_____
_____
_____
_____
_____
_____
_____
_____
_____

PERFECTION

THE ANOINTING IS PERFECTION, NOT THE PERSON!
We must stop trying to hold both to the same standards.

1 JOHN 2:20

Take a moment and reflect on today's word before journaling.

_____

_____

_____

_____

_____

_____

_____

_____

_____

_____

_____

_____

_____

_____

_____

_____

_____

_____

_____

_____

_____

_____

_____

_____

Day 79

INSTRUCTION

As Christians, we will not always get it right. Our gracious and merciful Father has already given us instructions on how to move forward. Dusk yourself off, repent, and proceed.

2 CHRONICLES 7:14

Did the Holy Spirit speak to that place in your heart?

_____
_____
_____
_____
_____
_____
_____
_____
_____
_____
_____
_____
_____
_____
_____
_____
_____
_____
_____
_____
_____
_____

NEVER

Never let the faithlessness of others
determine how you proceed.

Stay Connected to the Vine for ALL your Directions!

PSALM 28:7

What did the Holy Spirit reveal to you from this reading?

_____

_____

_____

_____

_____

_____

_____

_____

_____

_____

_____

_____

_____

_____

_____

_____

_____

_____

_____

_____

_____

SEEDS

Father, may my offerings of my time, talent, and treasure be acceptable
in your sight. May I forever bless and worship the
giver of my seeds which is you O, God.
In Jesus Name, Amen!

1 CORINTHIANS 3:6

Read and reflect on this scripture today as you journal.

_____

_____

_____

_____

_____

_____

_____

_____

_____

_____

_____

_____

_____

_____

_____

_____

_____

_____

_____

_____

_____

_____

_____

SHIELD

Thank you, God, for Your way is perfect; Your word Lord is
proven; You are a shield to all who trust in You.
May I never take my eyes off you.
In Jesus Name. Amen.

PSALM 18:30

Were you comforted by this word?

_____

_____

_____

_____

_____

_____

_____

_____

_____

_____

_____

_____

_____

_____

_____

_____

_____

_____

_____

_____

Day 83

MEDITATE

Today I will discipline myself to meditate for 5 minutes on the fullness of God and how He is showing Himself mighty in my life through His Word.

PHILIPPIANS 4:8

Your thoughts, prayers, or questions about this time with the Lord;

_____

_____

_____

_____

_____

_____

_____

_____

_____

_____

_____

_____

_____

_____

_____

_____

_____

_____

_____

_____

_____

_____

_____

ACKNOWLEDGE

**The unbelievers and the wicked too must bow
and acknowledge God!**

It is written:
"'As surely as I live, says the Lord, every knee will bow before me;
every tongue will acknowledge God.
ROMANS 14:11

What did the Holy Spirit reveal to you from this reading?

_____

_____

_____

_____

_____

_____

_____

_____

_____

_____

_____

_____

_____

_____

_____

_____

_____

_____

_____

_____

_____

BINDS

Still yourself before the Lord and allow Him to mend
every broken area in your life as only He can!
In the Name of Jesus. Amen.

He heals the brokenhearted and binds up their wounds.
PSALM 147:3

Were you comforted by this word?

_____

_____

_____

_____

_____

_____

_____

_____

_____

_____

_____

_____

_____

_____

_____

_____

_____

_____

_____

_____

_____

_____

Day 86

CHALLENGE

Today I challenge you to donate your
time, talent, or treasure to someone or something.

HEBREWS 10:24-25

Were you comfortable with the challenge? Why or why not?

_____

_____

_____

_____

_____

_____

_____

_____

_____

_____

_____

_____

_____

_____

_____

_____

_____

_____

_____

_____

_____

_____

SOMEBODY

I WILL BE ONE WHO MAKES EVERYBODY
FEEL LIKE SOMEBODY!

LUKE 6:31

What did you learn about yourself from this word?

_____

_____

_____

_____

_____

_____

_____

_____

_____

_____

_____

_____

_____

_____

_____

_____

_____

_____

_____

_____

_____

_____

_____

_____

_____

_____

Day 88

RESCUE

Jesus came to seek and save the lost!
He uses broken people like you and me
to rescue broken people like you and me!

LUKE 19:10

What did the Holy Spirit reveal to you from this reading?

_____

_____

_____

_____

_____

_____

_____

_____

_____

_____

_____

_____

_____

_____

_____

_____

_____

_____

_____

_____

_____

_____

JESUS

JESUS IS ALIVE EVERY DAY!
Don't wait for a special occasion to visit Him!

PSALM 112:6-8

Share this word with a friend today after you've journaled.

_____

_____

_____

_____

_____

_____

_____

_____

_____

_____

_____

_____

_____

_____

_____

_____

_____

_____

_____

_____

_____

_____

_____

Day 90

MEDITATE

Today I will discipline myself to meditate for 5 minutes on the fullness of God
and how He is showing Himself mighty in my life through His Word.

PHILIPPIANS 4:8

Your thoughts, prayers or questions about this time with the Lord;

_____

_____

_____

_____

_____

_____

_____

_____

_____

_____

_____

_____

_____

_____

_____

_____

_____

_____

_____

_____

_____

_____

_____

_____

PLANTED

Father, as I draw near to the end of this experience, I have gotten rid of
all moral filth and the evil that is so prevalent and I have humbly
accepted the word planted in me, which can save me.
In the Name of Jesus. Amen.

JAMES 1:21

Did the Holy Spirit speak to that place in your heart where you are struggling?

_____

_____

_____

_____

_____

_____

_____

_____

_____

_____

_____

_____

_____

_____

_____

_____

_____

_____

_____

_____

_____

_____

_____

Day 92

STEPPING

Heavenly Father, thank you for being with me as I read, studied, mediated, memorized, and challenged myself over the last 364 days. Father, I am Stepping into my NEXT redeemed, refreshed, renewed, and revived with fresh fire. Thank you, Father, that as I continue on my journey that your word will always be before me to lead, protect, and teach me. In the Name of Jesus. Amen.

ISAIAH 43:18-19

How did this word speak to you today?

_____

_____

_____

_____

_____

_____

_____

_____

_____

_____

_____

_____

_____

_____

_____

_____

_____

_____

_____

INDEX OF READING

DAY 1	ASSIGNMENT	PSALM 103:10-14
DAY 2	CHALLENGE	HEBREWS 10:24-25
DAY 3	THIRST	PSALM 63:3
DAY 4	SUSTAIN	PSALM 51:12-13
DAY 5	CONTINUOUSLY	LUKE 4:8
DAY 6	MEDITATE	PHILIPPIANS 4:8
DAY 7	DISCERN	1 JOHN 4:1
DAY 8	WILL	PSALM 40:8
DAY 9	POWER	2 CORINTHIANS 4:7
DAY 10	ENLIGHTENED	EPHESIANS 1:18
DAY 11	BETTER	PSALM 63:3
DAY 12	TRICKS	1 PETER 5:8-9
DAY 13	MEDITATE	PHILIPPIANS 4:8
DAY 14	SEEK	1 PETER 3:8-12
DAY 15	GLORY	PROVERBS 27:2
DAY 16	CHALLENGE	HEBREWS 10:24-25
DAY 17	PERFECT	2 CORINTHIANS 12:9
DAY 18	DELIGHT	PSALM 119:43
DAY 19	SEE	PSALM 119:18
DAY 20	MEDITATE	PHILIPPIANS 4:8
DAY 21	HEARTACHE	MATTHEW 5:4
DAY 22	IMPERFECT	EXODUS 34:6-7
DAY 23	CHAINED	2 TIMOTHY 2:9
DAY 24	HYPOCRITES	MATTHEW 15:19
DAY 25	ABUNDANCE	PROVERBS 3:10
DAY 26	ENTER	PSALM 100:1-5
DAY 27	MEDITATE	PHILIPPIANS 4:8
DAY 28	FEAR	ISAIAH 11:3
DAY 29	WHATEVER	COLOSSIANS 3:17
DAY 30	CHALLENGE	HEBREWS 10:24-25
DAY 31	THANKS	PSALM 136:1-3
DAY 32	WORK	JOHN 9:4
DAY 33	LIE	NUMBERS 23:19
DAY 34	MEDITATE	PHILIPPIANS 4:8
DAY 35	REWARD	MATTHEW 6:3-4
DAY 36	FRUIT	LUKE 12:48
DAY 37	JUDGE	1 CORINTHIANS 11:31
DAY 38	ANOINTING	JOHN 14:6
DAY 39	BORN	JOHN 3:5-6
DAY 40	MASTER	ROMANS 6:14
DAY 41	MEDITATE	PHILIPPIANS 4:8
DAY 42	FLESH	GALATIANS 5:17-21
DAY 43	WILDERNESS	ISAIAH 43:19
DAY 44	CHALLENGE	HEBREWS 10:24-25
DAY 45	ABOVE	PSALM 143:8
DAY 46	PLANS	JEREMIAH 29:11
DAY 47	TELL	1 JOHN 3:18

DAY 48	MEDITATE	PHILIPPIANS 4:8
DAY 49	TREASURE	MATTHEW 6:19-21
DAY 50	SOUL	1 KINGS 8:61
DAY 51	REST	1 CORINTHIANS 9:24
DAY 52	REVENGE	ROMANS 12:19
DAY 53	FOOLS	PROVERBS 18:6-7
DAY 54	NARROW	MATTHEW 7:13-14
DAY 55	MEDITATE	PHILIPPIANS 4:8
DAY 56	PREPARED	1 CORINTHIANS 2:9
DAY 57	PURSUE	PROVERBS 21:21
DAY 58	CHALLENGE	HEBREWS 10:24-25
DAY 59	OPINION	JOHN 8:32
DAY 60	JUDGEMENTAL	MATTHEW 7:2
DAY 61	DESTROYED	2 CORINTHIANS 4:7-10
DAY 62	MEDITATE	PHILIPPIANS 4:8
DAY 63	LESSON	ROMANS 8:28
DAY 64	SEPARATE	ROMANS 8:38-39
DAY 65	SERVE	ROMANS 12:1
DAY 66	BECOMING	PHILIPPIANS 1:6
DAY 67	HOPE	ISAIAH 40:31
DAY 68	CLOTHED	ISAIAH 61:10
DAY 69	MEDITATE	PHILIPPIANS 4:8
DAY 70	COVER	**HEBREWS 11:6**
DAY 71	COUNSEL	ISAIAH 11:2
DAY 72	CHALLENGE	HEBREWS 10:24-25
DAY 73	SECURE	PSALM 34:4-5
DAY 74	DEEP	LUKE 12:2
DAY 75	FREE	2 CORINTHIANS 3:17
DAY 76	MEDITATE	PHILIPPIANS 4:8
DAY 77	JOYFUL	ROMANS 12:12
DAY 78	PERFECTION	1 JOHN 2:20
DAY 79	INSTRUCTION	2 CHRONICLES 7:14
DAY 80	NEVER	PSALM 28:7
DAY 81	SEEDS	1 CORINTHIANS 3:6
DAY 82	SHIELD	PSALM 18:30
DAY 83	MEDITATE	PHILIPPIANS 4:8
DAY 84	ACKNOWLEDGE	ROMANS 14:11
DAY 85	BINDS	PSALM 147:3
DAY 86	CHALLENGE	HEBREWS 10:24-25
DAY 87	SOMEBODY	LUKE 6:31
DAY 88	RESCUE	LUKE 19:10
DAY 89	JESUS	PSALM 112:6-8
DAY 90	MEDITATE	PHILIPPIANS 4:8
DAY 91	PLANTED	JAMES 1:21
DAY 92	STEPPING	ISAIAH 43:18-19

WEBSITE

wordofthedaybook.com

EMAIL

wordofthedaybook@gmail.com

All parts can also be purchased on Amazon.com

AVAILABLE NOW ALL 365 DAYS

HAPPY JOURNALING!